PORT
~ AUTHORITY

PORT AUTHORITY

CONOR MCPHERSON

THEATRE COMMUNICATIONS GROUP
NEW YORK

Port Authority is published by Theatre Communications Group, Inc.,
355 Lexington Ave., New York, NY 10017-6603.

Port Authority is published in arrangement with Nick Hern Books Limited, 14 Larden Rd., London, England W3 7ST.

This publication is made possible in part with public funds from the New York State Council on the Arts, a State Agency.

TCG books are exclusively distributed to the book trade by Consortium Book Sales and Distribution, 1045 Westgate Dr., St. Paul, MN 55114.

LIBRARY OF CONGRESS CATALOGING-IN-PUBLICATION DATA

McPherson, Conor 1971–
Port Authority / by Conor McPherson.—1st ed.
p. cm.
ISBN 1-55936-207-3 (alk. paper)
1. Dublin (Ireland)—Drama. I. Title.
PR6063.C73 P67 2001
822'.914—dc21   2001045686

Cover, book design and typography by Lisa Govan

First edition, November 2002

PORT
AUTHORITY

PRODUCTION HISTORY

Port Authority was first produced by the Gate Theatre,
Dublin, at the New Ambassadors Theatre, London, in
association with Ambassador Theatre Group and Old Vic
Productions on February 22, 2001. The play opened at the
Gate Theatre, Dublin, on April 24, 2001. The director was
Conor McPherson, set design and costumes were by Eileen
Diss and the lighting design was by Mick Hughes. The cast,
in order of appearance, was:

KEVIN	Éanna MacLiam
DERMOT	Stephen Brennan
JOE	Jim Norton

CHARACTERS

Kevin, *maybe twenty*
Dermot, *late thirties? mid-thirties?*
Joe, *seventy-odd*

AUTHOR'S NOTE

The play is set in the theatre.

1

KEVIN

I moved out in the summer.

The house was in Donnycarney and four of us were going to share it.

My folks were not happy about it.

The mad thing was I could see their point.

It was kind of stupid.

I had no job and I didn't know what I wanted to do.

Moving out was like pretending to make a decision.

My dad gave me a lift down to Donnycarney.

With all my clothes in black bin-liners.

It was a bright Sunday afternoon.

I nearly said, "I'll see you later."

But this was supposed to be for good.

What a joke.

I was moving in with Davy Rose and a guy called Speedy.

I was mates with Davy.

To everybody else in Dublin he was Mad Davy Rose, hammered on Scrumpy Jack.

But I saw the normal side to him and he spoke to me about stuff and, you know?

Speedy was more Davy's friend than mine.

Although I could hardly see how anyone could be friends with Speedy at all.

He always seemed to me to be unbelievably stupid.

He definitely had a learning disorder or something.

Mostly he was just out of it, but even sober I couldn't make head nor tail of him.

It was like he was excited by being bored.

I had nothing in common with him.

He was asleep in the back garden when I went through.

Davy was sitting in an old deckchair, drinking cider and playing Billy Idol on his ghettoblaster.

He was in a state of agitation because he was in the process of being dumped by this girl with blue hair from Beaumount.

He was all distracted, talking about hopping on his bike going up to annoy her.

I didn't want him to leave me on my own with Speedy so I made him come down to the off-license with me and I got us more Scrumpy.

And we just went back and kept drinking.

Davy was searching through Speedy's pockets for smokes and I was casually inquiring where Clare was.

She was moving in as well.

Everybody in Dublin was in love with her.

She was buds with me and Davy but she tended to go out with headbangers. Or lads who thought they were, anyway.

She was always with some spiky-haired crusty who you could see was from Dublin 4 or somewhere, putting on a bit of an accent.

They were all rich and spoiled and better looking than any of us.

Davy said he hadn't seen her.

So we got fairly pissed there in the garden and then I went up to see which room was mine.

I had the bedroom at the back.

Davy had the attic conversion.

Clare had the bedroom at the front.

Speedy was in the boxroom.

We were all paying thirty quid, except Speedy who was paying twenty.

All was in my room was a bed and a chair.

I was in my sleeping bag all night lying there awake listening to hear if I could Clare come in but all I could hear were all the sounds that made me try to imagine I was still at home.

But it didn't work.

In the morning I borrowed Davy's bike and I went down to Kilbarrack to sign on and sort out rent allowance.

And when I got back it was just Speedy sitting there watching Richard and Judy.

He nodded at me and I sat down there near him.

But he was genuinely watching Richard and Judy.

I was nearly afraid to say anything in case he missed something.

He was eating Rice Krispies like he was on his way out to work in a minute or something.

As if, you know.

And he suddenly starts saying, still not looking at me, about how last Friday a guy from a band from Donaghmede had called down with this small goth girl who was a notorious slut.

And your man was in the back room with Davy jamming on these two basses that were in there.

And your one asks Speedy if his has any hash and he had so they went up to the boxroom and had a spliff and all of a sudden they got stuck into each other, having a sneaky ride.

And Speedy was trying to listen out to hear if he could still hear your man jamming with Davy and he wasn't coming up. But your one was starting to make so much noise that Speedy just got too nervous so he just went into the jacks and pulled himself off.

And he said all this to me just like that.

And I was just sitting there staring at the side of his head, thinking that there was nothing he could ever say that could interest me beyond the terrible notion that I cared absolutely nothing for this fellow human being. And that if he died I'd feel nothing.

And we sat there in this room for a while until I could barely stand it.

Until I casually asked him if he knew when Clare was moving in.

But there was nothing about Speedy to suggest that anyone had just spoken to him.

And I was trying to decide whether to ask him again or just fuck off out or something and he just goes, "She's here."

2

DERMOT

Dinner. Friday night. O'Hagan's house.

A kind of a welcome to the fold.

And the elation of a huge salary in an interesting job and having impressed these clean-shaven tailor-made suits was clashing with the embarrassment of having to present Mary to them.

Suddenly I was thinking about my wife.

It was all right when I was at Whelan's.

All the wives looked the same.

Down at the Christmas do in the Old Sheiling.

We moaned about them at the bar.

The way they were squealing at each other.

Hysterical, at being out of the house.

Just a few weeks before I'd been looking for some old accountancy textbooks in the press in the bedroom and a load of chocolate fell out on top of me.

And I just didn't even bother, you know that way?

She took up half the couch and watched *EastEnders*.

And I sat in the boxroom brushing up for the interview.

O'Hagan had rang me himself personally to tell me I'd got it.

Cocktails in Gogarty's Monday night to say hello.

Griffen, Staunton, Crawford. Strong handshakes.

What I presumed was Armani. All ex-rugby.

And then one or two of their wives suddenly.

And I was like, "Holy fuck, easy tiger!"

Me in my Penny's blazer and my loafers from Dunnes.

Hardly able, but trying to swallow these Glenmorangies being pressed into my fist.

Swaying in the door.

Mary and Colm curled up in the living room watching *Friends*.

Colm. Nine years of age. Constant cold.

Useless at sports.

Bullied until third class.

Until Mary went down and spoke to the head.

Went down on her own.

Because there was simply only so much I could fit in.

And the head dealt with it.

And I drove Mary and Colm wherever they wanted to go at the weekends, and although I wouldn't say I was necessarily a quiet person, I hardly said a fucking word.

Dinner in O'Hagan's house. Friday night.

I whined at Mary about how I needed to dress better.

She took me from shop to shop and I shelled out for three suits. Cotton shirts. Silk ties.

Catching Mary smiling and seeing what there was to see in her when we were younger, but we weren't younger now and I told her that dinner at O'Hagan's was staff only.

No wives. That was another night.

And for once I had something to treasure, that I was looking forward to.

A glittering jewel on the mountain at the top of Friday.

And me trudging towards it not wanting to get there too quickly.

Enjoying it in the middle distance.

Because I could see it and it was mine.

And it was going to happen.

3

JOE

Sister Pat knocked while I was getting dressed.

I could smell breakfast being served.

It was the first morning I'd felt hungry in ages.

She had a little box wrapped in brown paper.

It was addressed to me, but at my son's house.

His wife, Lisa, had dropped it in to me on her way to work.

Sister Pat was the closest thing I had to a friend, really.

She was the same age as a lot of the residents but like that old expression, young at heart.

As opposed to me who was just bloody immature.

"It's not your birthday or something, is it?" she says.

"No, my birthday's not 'til June," I go.

My birthday's not 'til June! Like it'd make a difference!

Sure I hadn't had a birthday present in years, sure!

Who'd be sending an old curmudgeon birthday presents?

And not on his birthday.

I'm not that popular.

Well. I felt like a bit of a twit standing there holding it.

It was very light. But there was definitely something in it.

For a religious, Sister Pat had a lot of little girl in her.

She was being nosey, standing there waiting for me to open it. But, like the bold child she knew she was, she knew I was too awkward to tell her to clear off the hell there out of it.

"Are you not going to open it?" she goes.

"I am," I say.

Little box covered in brown paper.

Dun Laoghaire postmark.

"I'm going to wait 'til I have my breakfast," I say.

"And I'll open it when I'm drinking my tea."

"Do you know what you are?" she says to me.

"You're very vain."

And she left then.

I knew what she meant, but she said things like that and there was no real anger in it.

And it didn't really make me feel anything really either.

That's just what she was like.

Very direct.

A brilliant nun really.

A perfect bloody nun.

So I put on my jacket and took my stick and I went down the corridor to the dining room.

There was about twenty of us in the home at that point.

Quick look around.

All present and correct.

No one gone up to Beaumont in the middle of the night.

A few of us had sticks.

And a few were in wheelchairs.

But we were fairly agile now, not too bad.

I sat down there beside Jackie Fennel and Mary Larkin.

Who I mostly sat with when I ate.

Often me and Jackie'd wander round to the bookies and get a bottle of stout in Tighe's.

And we'd put little bets on for Mary Larkin as well.

Local women worked in the home and they made you your breakfast and they brought it over to you and everything.

They were great to us.

So there we were and we spoke about the weather and Mary Larkin's son, Peter, who was a guard and whose wife was expecting another baby.

And Jackie Fennel was looking at the racing in the *Independent*.

And now and again I'd think about the little box in my pocket. And my arm'd move a little bit.

And after breakfast when everyone began to mooch off for a chat or do their own thing, I sat there by myself having a cup of tea while the local women cleared up.

And I took out the box and I pulled at the string which I put in my pocket.

And I pulled the paper off neatly because it was all done neatly and I figured out how to get into the cardboard.

And there was a little handwritten note and something flat wrapped in tissue paper.

I pulled it out and I took away the tissue.

It was a small photo that I recognized.

And I knew what had happened and I didn't need to read the note.

~ 4

KEVIN

Clare was sticking luminous stars up on the wall and ceiling of her room.

She wanted to paint the walls.

I said I didn't think we'd be let.

She said this was like a room where you sent your granny to die.

Clare was very much sort of up to the minute.

When you saw her it took you a second but you knew she was special.

She cared about her appearance but in a very discreet way.

She wore makeup but you couldn't see it.

She was definitely sexy but at the same time she was one of the gang and very easy to be with.

For me anyway. And she saw me as like her mate.

Only when you saw her with a lot of other girls was she like . . . a girl.

I was never one of those guys who hung around with a lot of girls, as my friends.

If I knew a girl she was either the girlfriend of someone I knew, or it was someone I was going out with.

So me and Clare was a weird thing for me.

So I was usually thinking about it a lot.

And wondering if . . . you know.

I was putting a plug on her CD player for her and I was looking through her CDs.

She told me to take a tape out of a box beside her bed. It was a demo tape. The guy she was seeing was in a band.

Who wasn't? Everybody I knew was in half-assed bands.

Davy was in The Bangers.

He couldn't really play, but none of those bands were any use.

I'd always have to go into their gigs in pubs in town.

There'd be six bands on, and then like a really drunk
band at the end that wasn't really a band, just a mixture of
blokes from the other bands and some eejits who were just
their mates.

And they'd get up and try and play something by Fugazi or
someone, but because it was really hard and no one could
really play, they'd have to belt something easy out like
"Anarchy in the U.K."

These were pretty shite gigs now, you know? But I went
because all my mates were in that scene and you could have
a few beers and a bit of a laugh.

Everybody was a sort of a punk.

This was years after real punk.

But it was like a sub-grouping of people who weren't into
Bryan Adams or boy bands and all that.

I wasn't really a punk or anything.

I was just like one of their mates.

Guys like Davy who were notorious as mad bastards all over
Dublin. But who I saw the normal side of because we'd
grown up together and gone to school together and all that.

Clare's boyfriend's tape was in a case with a photocopied
cover in it.

I stuck it in the machine and I was slightly pissed off
because they actually sounded quite good.

They sounded like REM or someone.

"They're really good, aren't they?" Clare goes.

And I had to say yeah, they were.

They'd played support to some quite big bands like
The Lemonheads and The Jesus and Mary Chain.

"We should get The Bangers to play with them sometime,"
I said.

Clare said yeah. But wasn't like a real yeah, more like . . .
yeah! Bit too enthusiastic.

The Bangers were playing that night and we were going in to
see them so I went into my room while Clare got ready.

I hadn't unpacked any of my gear. I was pulling all my
clothes out but there was nowhere to put them, only on the
chair. So I put some trousers on the seat and some tops on
the back, and my trainers underneath.

And I stood back surveying this.

Thinking I had to get much more organized.

But who was I fooling. I was already useless.

Like I was starving and I'd no idea even if there was any food
in the house.

I heard the shower go on and I could hear Clare going, "Oh
my God!" at the state of the bathroom.

And later on we were down at the bus stop on the Malahide
Road.

It was a gorgeous summer's evening.

All amber and a cool breeze.

Clare had one of her runners off shaking a little stone out
of it.

I was leaning there looking at the mountains.

And Clare said up to me, she was kneeling on the ground,
"Are you all right?"

And I was looking at the mountains and nodding.

But I didn't think she could see me, so I said, "Yeah, I'm fine."

5

DERMOT

Den duh duh.

I was standing on the Dart.

There were plenty of seats but I don't know.

I couldn't sit.

I didn't need to.

All the kids in the latest gear.

Me. Okay older. Okay a bit pudgy.

But none of them had an idea where I was headed.

The windows were black, only a burst of orange in the stations or distant street lamps.

I was watching out for Sutton Cross.

Right there. On my own.

Holding on to a thing. A pole.

And people were getting on, getting off, whatever.

Not too busy because this was the opposite direction to town. But I was nicely oblivious because I was sort of plunging or something.

Banging right there into the peninsula from Raheny.

I kept looking up at the map. Like I didn't know.

Mary'd dropped me down to Raheny on her way to a hen night. And I walked straight over to the station until I saw her brakelights turn down at the village.

And I was back across over at the boozer like a shot.

Taking my time. Few little G&T's.

Few little ones in the afternoon as well.

At home while Mary was at the shops.

Before my shower.

Nice form. All the young loolas coming into the pub.

To spend the night here and wobble home, rowing with the girlfriend.

They could have it.

Three G&T's later I was down on the platform.

Nicely.

Standing there on the train. Up through Howth Junction.

Bayside.

Bang Bang.

Nearly missed fucking Sutton.

Off I hopped. Straight over to the Marine Hotel, no messing.

Had O'Hagan's address, but I needed a few directions.

Few G&T's later I felt fully equipped.

You can't ever go off half-cocked, half-medicated into uncharted waters, you'll be eaten alive.

O'Hagan's were one of, if not the most successful money managers in the country. They had all the big musicians and broadcasters and all the big writers and everyone. O'Hagan was a celebrity in his own right.

All the big fashion designers and all.

Christ knew who'd be up at this thing.

So I hung on to his gate for a few minutes snorting up any snot I wanted to get rid of, the sea stretching off towards the lights of the Southside.

And I was veering up his driveway, up to these steps going up to his door, thinking maybe I'd overdone it on the G&T's, 'cause there'd be plenty of booze inside, and I had this great revelation—that it was too fucking late to do anything about it now!

I didn't even care anymore.

So when I found the bell I gave it a right couple of rings to signal my confident arrival.

I was imagining church bells ringing out all across the country. And a little blondie yoke with no straps on her dress and her tits held up with wire opens the door and says, "Hello!"

"Hello!" I say, lobbing a leg over the threshold and yanking at the sleeve of my anorak.

"Everybody's here," she says.

"They are now!" says I.

And she doesn't really hear me and she carries my coat off into the house.

And it reminded me of when I was younger and my mum tried to get me into a posh school in Dublin run by the Jesuits. It was all wooden staircases and arched hallways. Did I get in?

Did I fuck!

She hadn't a notion, my mother.

And that's what this house was like.

Only all white. White on the walls and white funny carpet like a tight fishing net.

White little seats everywhere.

And a weird buzzing noise which I realized was people talking to each other.

And the blondie girl gives me champagne no less and brings me into the drawing room while I'm looking at her back.

But I don't know a sinner so I whore away at my glass and there's a tray with more and I take two.

And then, "Dermot!" It's fucking O'Hagan's wife.

Which is okay in itself.

But that she's basically wearing what looks to me like a piece of pink tissue paper and her tits are basically hanging out is giving me a problem.

And it's all see-through, but her tits are basically outside it and she's going, "How are you feeling?"

And I'm like yeah, yeah . . . Like I'm cool.

But the controllers in your head who are telling you that you have to live with your future self are filing this moment away under Moronic Moments To Relive Again And Again.

And for some reason I'm thinking about when I was nineteen and I used to cycle around on my sister's bike, and my clothes were old. Not old like you Saying Who You Were. But old like you'd had them a few years and the *fibers* were old in them. And they were all a bit gray and even though you didn't, you probably felt like you were probably into little girls. That you felt like you looked like you liked little girls.

And these thoughts were obviously evident in my face so O'Hagan's wife is saying, "Don't be intimidated!"

And she takes my arm and starts saying, "Come on, we're all going to eat now." And she's pulling me along and I feel like I'm going to go over on my snot so I'm walking all funny.

And then all of a sud we're going down a spiral staircase.

And then we're at the bottom and I'm like, "How the fuck did I manage that?" And sort of congratulating myself and I hear all this, "Dermot! Dermot! Over here!"

And there they all are. O'Hagan, Crawford, Staunton, all sitting down to eat rabbits while a woman like my mum is putting roast 'dates* down in a big flat bowl.

And Crawford is saying something like, "Dermot, don't ever be afraid of roast potatoes," or something.

And I go, "What the fuck are you saying?"

But nobody hears me.

*potatoes

32

And I feel a row coming on, but I'm on top of it.

And I think that I'll probably just break something later instead.

And the little blondie one seems to be in charge of everything.

But like she's been hired, at the same time she's like everyone's friend. And they all call her Charlotte and so do I because she's pumping the wine into everybody and constantly opening bottles.

And I realize that all the women at the table are like what I see in Mary's magazines.

All dressed like they always are, just before it all has to come off. Because it just has to.

And I'm watching Charlotte's severe fringe and the freckles across her nose and her tan, and O'Hagan's wife plunks down right opposite me.

And I try to distract myself by working out if we're on benches or seats, but if I check I'm a goner.

So I just silently place my hands on the table.

My head is the moon and I've got to keep it away from the earth.

I use my arms to do this.

And I use O'Hagan's wife's mostly visible tits to keep the astronauts from panicking.

33

We panic and we're gone.

So we're using O'Hagan's wife's tits as a vital NASA supply to balance our brains. Because we can, in our distraction, act automatically, and just use our reflexes, which are nature's cause-and-effect certainties.

And slowly I notice that everything has gone very quiet.

And I hear someone say, "Dermot?"

And I realize that someone must have just asked me a question.

And everyone's just twigged why the fuck I can't answer.

And O'Hagan's wife has a big reddener and she's got her napkin practically up at her neck.

And I have this overwhelming urge to use the toilet.

And not just use the toilet.

Use the fact that it has walls.

And that no one has X-ray eyes.

But of course they do, don't they?

Of course they fucking do.

6

JOE

I'm going to tell you something, right?

I was always just like everybody else.

Do you get me?

There was simply never any question about it.

You saw me with a bunch of people, you wouldn't notice me.

I never thought about myself.

I saw the world as a very organized place that was easy to negotiate. I saw people as generally good and if there were blackguards around the place— well that's what they were. Blackguards.

I met my wife, Liz, when I was working up in Cadbury's.

I was older than her and I'd sort of risen up through the ranks a bit by then and she was working on the floor.

Which made it a bit difficult to bump into her.

But I always had my eye on her. Don't know why.

She had thick little legs. She was small and a bit

. . . busty I suppose.

Got my chance to ask her up at the Christmas dance 1956.

To my astonishment she had no boyfriend and we started going out together.

I had a pretty flash car, an Austin, and I was still living with the parentals, so I had a few bob.

And Liz was basically a smasher in many ways.

Always laughing. Always in good form.

If there was an awkward silence, she just hummed to herself. Do you get me?

She was like me.

There was nothing neither wrong nor right about us.

I could easily stand in her parents' living room at Christmastime and she could easily sit in mine.

We got married in Cabra in 1960 and moved into a house in Donnycarney.

In those days in Ireland like, you didn't have a lot of the issues that you do now.

She cooked the dinner and packed in the job and I earned the spons. That was it. There was none of your everyone's on valium because they're all confused about who they are.

Listen, I'm not saying that things were better then than now, only different, and you didn't need to be asking all the questions you do now. And to tell you the truth that suited me. That suited me down to the ground. Because when the time came for me to have to start asking questions, let me tell you at the time,

I could've done without it.

Or maybe I'm glad it happened.

You see? I've no idea about myself!

I don't even know if I'm happy or sad!

But how and ever. Liz became pregnant with Stephen in '61. And two years later we had Tania.

Not a family name. Liz saw it in a film.

Oh, the times they were a changing, for sure.

And after a few years and the kids were that bit older and I was still earning a nice few bob, we decided to move to a bigger house.

A beautiful house up in Sutton.

Right there on the peninsula.

7

KEVIN

It was an absolutely dismal night for The Bangers.

It was the first time they'd headlined their own gig.

So they were paying for the rent on the venue and they'd had to hire the P.A.

There were supposed to be three bands, one of who, The Lepers, had a big following on their own.

But they'd had to cancel because one of them had lost a finger in the sheet metal factory where he worked.

Yeah, yeah, the jokes about the leper who'd lost his finger were endless.

A completely brutal band from Skerries were on.

It was ten o'clock and there were only about fifteen people in the place.

Davy was just getting hammered on Scrumpy Jack.

He had a bag of cans under the table.

He was talking about not going on.

Scampi, The Bangers' lead singer, was saying they might as well now they were here. Their guitar player, Vinnie Harper, said he couldn't give a shit either way.

Danny the drummer had shifted this small goth chick so he wasn't going anywhere.

It was lashing rain outside and the whole thing was just generally a bit depressing.

I was embarrassed for them as well because Clare had managed to drag her boyfriend along.

Not only was he a proper musician and actually worked, he had a job in a printers, he was actually a nice guy.

His name was Declan. Into that whole suede jacket, jeans and boots vibe.

Big sideburns on him.

And because Clare usually went out with terrible fucking morons I reckoned this might be the real thing.

She wasn't all over him or anything.

You could just tell she was into him.

Whenever he said anything, well you had to shout really at those gigs, she was right in there. Leaning in.

Giving him her ear. Nodding. Following him. Getting it, you know?

I was beginning to feel sick of the whole not-living-with-your-folks thing.

Clare couldn't stand Speedy. He was just constantly out of it. He was filthy and he always ate all her food.

It was a bad atmosphere.

Davy's genius solution was to have a big housewarming party to clear the air.

Without asking any of us he'd printed up flyers and fucking everyone in Dublin seemed to have one.

There was still two weeks to go and the word of mouth was becoming enormous.

I was seriously thinking about moving back home because basically it was going to be mental, the neighbors would definitely be calling the guards and the landlord who was a bit of a cunt anyway would have us all out on our snot in a heartbeat.

So there I was on this disastrous night for The Bangers and I was more or less lost in thought.

Davy had finally been persuaded to go on.

Vinnie Harper was only starting to tune up his guitar but Scampi just shouts, "We're The Bangers!"

And Davy just sort of jumped into the drum kit and they were away.

A couple of drunk crusties started moshing around a bit, but the truth was I'd never heard them sound worse.

Clare's boyfriend sat there with a stunned look of morbid interest. And me and Clare just looked at each other and burst out laughing. And I just went (*Mimes lifting glass to his mouth*) and she goes (*Thumbs up sign*).

So I wandered off downstairs to the empty bar.

Only little old men drank in here and it was dead.

I stood there staring up at an old photo of some priests holding up a big check and someone slapped me lightly across the face.

It was the girl working behind the counter.

She was my age and she had lots of curly hair.

"Wakey wakey," she goes.

I snapped out of it and asked her for two pints of Bulmers.

"You upstairs?" she asks me, sort of looking at me.

"Yeah," I said. "It's fucking awful."

And later on I was sitting in Jimmy Dean's diner with Clare and her boyfriend. And Davy was getting sick in the jacks.

And the barmaid who'd slapped me, whose name was Trish came in and joined us.

And I wasn't completely surprised.

Because when I'd asked her to she said she definitely might all right.

8

DERMOT

Don't ever try to work anything out.

Because you don't know—and you never will.

And even if you do, it'll be too late to do anything about it anyway.

Just don't bother. You'd think I'd been a disaster at O'Hagan's party?

A danger to shipping?

An embarrassment at the very least, ha?

A tableful of people had just watched me transfixed, I mean transported by my boss's wife's boobs.

A tableful of whatdoyoucallit, your colleagues.

But nothing was normal about this.

Are you normal?

'Cause if you think you are—you'll be like me.

Sitting on the toilet.

Clenching my fists and unclenching them.

Rocking back and forth.

Staring into the fact that I'd blown it.

Blown it all to hell up the wazoo.

Trying to ignore the little knocks at the door.

No one was going to throw me out. I'd leave of my own accord when I was good and ready, clutching the last shreds of my dignity on my own thank you very much.

But it was the way O'Hagan's wife said my name.

"Dermot?" she said. "Are you all right?"

The way she said it.

Through the door.

There was no punishment in it.

No judgment or something.

Unbelievably.

It made me open the door.

So I stood there and I started to say how sorry I was and too much to drink and so on.

But she just laughed a little sad laugh.

And placed a reassuring hand on my arm.

And I heard O'Hagan and the others shouting from the kitchen.

"Dermo!" O'Hagan was going. "Get yourself back in here and have your sweet, you fucking eejit!"

And I went back in there with his wife.

What is it? Money? Or royalty or something?

Where the rules are different.

But I should have twigged that something was weird about all this ages before.

Right there in the beginning.

At the interview.

I mean, I don't think they even asked me about three questions. Three maybe. And they were like general what do you make of the present state of affairs as they stand at the moment type questions.

Rhetorical, even, like, "Who can say what way the bloody country is going, ha?"

I mean, how do you answer?

You know?

You sort of go, "Well, it's very hard to say, isn't it?" That's all I could do.

And O'Hagan just goes, "Well everything we've heard about you is very impressive, and we'll be in touch."

Heard what about me?

That I'd never actually passed my ACCA?

Or that in the eighteen months I'd worked in Denis Mahony's I never sold a single car? Not one!

Or what, that I'd been sacked out of Whelan's for so-called sexual harassment? Of, supposedly, another man!

What? That I was just generally a bit of a disaster?

Whatever they'd heard, I wasn't going to question it!

They'd given me the job and here I was.

I mean I sat back down there at the table and I was *totally* accepted.

And I hadn't even started working yet, you know?

Well, what the fuck.

Here were coming the cigars and I took one and someone else's wife lit it for me.

And O'Hagan comes down beside me.

His big arm around my shoulders.

"You're a man after my own heart," he goes. "Ha? Ha?"

Me smiling and nodding, pretending I know what the fuck is going on.

And then he goes, "You ever heard of The Bangers?"

Had I what?

They were the biggest thing out of Ireland since The Cranberries. They were going to be as big as U2.

Huge in the States.

"We look after them," he says. "They're kicking off their tour in Los Angeles St. Patrick's weekend. We're all going to go. Are you free?" he says to me.

Well it was that or 'round to Mary's mother's house for corned beef and cabbage and rock-hard potatoes.

So I thought about it.

For about a millisecond.

The big blank head on me.

9

JOE

You want a tip?

When you dream in the night, just wake up, forget about it, get on with it, get up in the morning and have your breakfast and go to work.

Be courteous in your job and use your manners.

'Cause if you dream that someone's loving you and you wake up looking for them and sending signals to all and sundry around you in the daytime, saying, "Was it you? Was it you who loved me?"

You'll fucking find them, mark my words.

They'll come to you.

They'll seem different.

Like someone who's changed over the years like you knew them as a child. But it'll be them.

And all that longing that's in you.

When you thought you'd never meet again and a dam bursts.

It's all in you.

And for an ordinary man like me to discover that.

Well it was slightly the end of the world there for a little while.

What happened was this.

When we moved up to the peninsula, up to Sutton, our nextdoor neighbors invited us into a party in their house one Saturday night.

His name was Tommy Ross and his wife's name was Marion.

They were having a family do.

It was Tommy's parents' anniversary and they were throwing a bit of a bash.

I'd only ever chatted to him a little bit maybe in the garden in the morning. I'd never spoken to her.

Liz, my wife, had tended to stay friendly with her old pals from Cadbury's and from where we'd lived in Donnycarney.

Stephen was ten and Tania was eight.

Naturally, they fought like tigers, so even though we were only going next door for a few hours, Liz's sister, Aunty Carmel, came up to baby-sit and we were able to go.

And even though we didn't know anyone at all, you see in those days you just spoke to people.

Even though then it was like it is now and people had a few bob.

We'd bought a table set for Tom's parents and we chatted to them for a while.

And I spoke to one of Tom's brothers, Frank, and his wife, Phyllis, and Liz was chatting to another sister, Bernie.

And it was all very pleasant.

In those days I drank bottles of Smithwicks.

And there was all six-packs of Smithwicks and Guinness and Harp all stacked up in the garage, and all the nieces and nephews'd bring some in and take out the empties and all this and it was about ten o'clock and very pleasant.

The first one or two early risers might have started to leave, but things were more or less in full swing.

And I went into the kitchen at one point to get myself another ham sandwich or an egg sandwich, and I got talking to Tom Ross's wife, Marion, and as we'd never really spoken before, it was only natural that we should fill in a lot of history, being new neighbors.

Now before you start thinking, Yo ho! Here's where it gets good!, let me explain that there were other people in the kitchen and this was all normal and acceptable.

Only, the night before I'd had a dream that I was down at this river and there was a woman there with jet black hair and the unconditional no-nonsense acceptance I'd felt was like, when I woke up, that I'd lost a part of myself.

Not that Marion looked anything like this woman in the dream.

She looked nothing like her.

She had short fair hair and a little pug nose.

And she was telling me about the people who'd lived next door before we moved in and how horrible they were, and I was just staring at her for some reason and the strange way she twisted her jaw when she became full of good-humored bad thoughts about people she was criticizing.

And I was desperately trying to cop onto myself.

And eat this bloody ham sandwich, but there was no water in my mouth so I was drinking too much Smithwicks.

But it all seemed so bloody unimportant when I watched her little leg spin whenever she heard a song she liked come on.

So I made sure we made our way out to the living room and I stood there with my arm on Liz for the rest of the night.

With everyone, including Marion, oblivious of what had just happened to me.

And me putting it all out of my mind hopelessly as a passing nonsense that'd do nobody any good in the long run.

And you fool yourself that God hasn't seen you.

But there were a few little involuntary twitches in my legs and hands for the next hour or two until we went to bed, let me tell you!

. . . I put it down to the drink.

And of course to that bloody dream I'd had.

And that was the end of that.

But, of course it was impossible for him not to, God had seen me.

10

KEVIN

I had a comfortable time then.

Trish was a student at NCAD.

And she worked in the pub in the evenings.

I was like a little old man there.

Going in. Sitting up there watching the snooker.

Having a pint or two.

She lived around the corner in a flat on Parliament Street.

We fucked all night all the time.

She'd shake her head, all her curly hair hitting me in the face.

All her pent-up frustrations about being from the country.

Her legs around mine so I couldn't get away.

The condom coming off and bursting and every fucking thing.

She didn't speak to me much though.

Not about anything important.

You even looked at her too long, I mean admiringly, she'd come straight over and punch you in the chest, wanting to know what you were staring at.

But other things like, you'd be standing there in the Spar buying a can of Coke and her hand would slip into mine, absent-mindedly, and automatic, no strings attached, just proper love.

The light blazing across her face when we were sitting on the bus, upstairs at the front.

Going out through Fairview up to Donnycarney.

She loved Davy.

They were the same.

They wanted more than the world had to give them.

She drank and dragged me to my feet to dance, her hand clamped on my arse.

Clare was confused by her a bit I think.

And, maybe it was because, all of a sud, here was something me and Clare couldn't talk about.

All of us there hanging round the house.

Clare giving Davy a hard time about the whole of Dublin being invited to the housewarming.

Davy in a stupor.

Speedy mostly asleep.

I was watching *The Simpsons* and I got up to make a cup of coffee.

And Trish and Clare were standing there in the kitchen talking, and I moved between them like I wasn't welcome.

Like I needed a friend.

And we went down to the pub and Trish got up to get a round, and I was eating some crisps and I caught Clare looking at me and we started laughing.

Well it was that or bursting into tears or some fucking thing.

Later on in the chipper Clare began to get organized about we had to go to the supermarket the next day because if Davy wasn't going to do anything about this party, then we had to.

Trish was pretending her battered sausage was someone's dick. She only had a gray vest top on.

And later on she gave me the most unbelievable blow job.

I nearly came all over the place.

You see someone laughing with your spunk all over them, let's face it you're on to a good thing.

All in her curly hair and all.

And that night we fell asleep together for the first time.

She was late for college and everything.

I had my jeans on and I was eating cornflakes there in my bare feet and Clare comes into the kitchen twirling car keys on her finger.

She'd borrowed her mam's Fiesta.

And we drove down to Superquinn in Sutton Cross.

She had a silver bracelet on her left arm and she had a tan and I was watching it when she changed gears.

And projecting ahead like we were married and this was what we did all the time.

The little concentrated look on her face going up through the traffic.

Her thin lips at all the bad drivers.

And I'd never done anything like this except with my mum, pushing a trolley around the supermarket.

I just wanted to grab Clare right there.

She had sporty stripes down her pants.

She had no socks on.

And just, her stupid ankles there.

Like she'd never need to wear socks if she was with me or something.

Obviously I was losing it, so I clamped my fingers around the handle on the trolley.

And we both knew this housewarming thing was going to be disastrous.

And I began to realize that Clare had to know there was no point in buying stuff for a bunch of mentlers who were going to come and just basically drink you out of house and home.

And I knew that all this supermarket bullshit was because Clare just wanted to spend some time with me again.

And she turned at one point and put her hand on my belly while we were looking at frozen pizzas.

And for ages we couldn't move.

11

DERMOT

First class on a plane?

To America?

It's all napkins and tablecloths and, "You were drinking the chardonnay, sir?"

It's stupid.

I don't know how much it costs, but we're talking thousands, yeah?

And it was St. Patrick's weekend, so they were all there.

Adams, McGuinness, Reynolds, Cowan, Ahern, Eammon Dunphy, Ian Dempsey and me, and O'Hagan and Crawford Griffen, Staunton, and all their wives.

But no Mary.

She'd stood there in the shadow and the light there on the landing, my hand on hers on the banister.

"I have to go," I said, "they're making me."

And fuck, she saw right through me.

She didn't say a fucking word.

But she'd clocked me.

I was snared.

But where do you go?

You stay where you are.

And she nodded and smiled and went off into the bathroom.

And I used the sound of the bath running to open the drinks cabinet and help myself to some strange cocktail which kicked in a little while later while I was lying on the sofa thinking about L.A.

And here I was!

On the broom broom.

And we're all getting up and walking around like we're in a club or something.

Meeting and greeting. Pressing the flesh.

With the great and the good.

The air hostesses all licking up to us, everybody laughing at everybody else's stupid comments.

But nothing could hide that there was a bit of a smell of shit on the plane, like one of the jacks was broken or something.

A smell to which I have to say I contributed to with a couple of hefty pounds of crap myself.

It goes in, it comes out!

What are you going to do? Hold it in?

I stank up my bloody hotel room first thing as well.

We'd all been picked up by limos.

I was knackered and fairly drunk from the plane.

And The Bangers' concert was that night.

"Don't go asleep, Dermot," they were all warning me, "the only way to beat the jet lag is to stay up."

Stay up! I felt like it was half-eleven at night and I'd been in the pub all day.

Stay up . . .

I sat there on the bed in the hotel.

I had a load of rooms. One like a sitting room.

One for like having your nosh or to hold a meeting in. And one like a proper hotel room with a bed. Me in the middle. The stinky smell of my crap all over the place.

Mary'd packed this pair of shorts she'd got me.

They were like cool combat shorts with big pockets on the side of them.

So I put them on and went down looking for the bar.

But at reception they told me the bar didn't open until like six or something ridiculous.

So I wandered back up to my room and I sat on the balcony looking down into the empty pool, and I made a right few dents into the minibar until the phone finally rang and it was time to go down to the lobby where we were all meeting our limo to take us to see The Bangers.

But in truth we weren't going to see The Bangers.

We were going to The Bangers' concert which is different.

We were going to be backstage in the VIP enclosure.

All O'Hagan and them and their wives all dressed casual, all hip and laid back and not millionaires, all in their brand-new sparkling white Nikes.

So if you said to me, "What are The Bangers like live?" I couldn't tell you.

But I can tell you that backstage is like something out of *Lord of the Rings*.

You can see the stage and the speakers towering up and all banners blowing in the wind like a castle and a little village of people all milling around. All hoping that some rubbish is going to be thrown out of the castle one day, and by mistake there'll be something good in it, like a diamond, and if you're the one that finds it you're never going to have to work again or ever be hungry anymore.

I was beginning to feel scared and the night air was cold and I was trying to numb all my fears by drinking vodka. And I got talking to some blond girl and her husband. He was English and on the off chance that I was someone important they were being very friendly towards me. And they asked me if I wanted to take some cocaine.

I'd never taken it in my life but I wanted anything to take away these scary feelings I was having.

So we snorted this cocaine up our noses in a portaloo.

The smell of shit was overwhelming and a roar went up from eighty thousand people and I spun out into the night, quite convinced that bats were going to attack me.

And I had a bottle of vodka in my hand and I cowered in the corner of a field, feeling that my life was in great danger.

Until O'Hagan's wife found me and we went to some party where I couldn't stay and the next thing I knew I was back in the hotel room.

It had started to get bright.

I had my shorts on and I was looking at the weird dimples on this girl's breast implants where it looked all plastic.

And I was on the phone and I was talking to Mary.

She was down there in Artane at her parents' house on the estate. She was on her mobile, and nieces and nephews were arriving for St. Patrick's Day.

I could hear them squealing.

She was standing there in the garden and I could imagine it.

All the sounds were all so innocent and somehow very real. There was an echo which struck me as something to do with the summer and I couldn't take it anymore so I said, "Take it easy." And I put the phone down.

And this girl on the bed was asleep and I was looking at her vagina and wondering how old she was and who she was, it was a plump dark line, and I was wondering if this funny feeling of the carpet under my feet was a feeling of remorse.

And I began to go asleep and the sun was beginning to shriek in the windows.

And then later, O'Hagan was in the room and the girl seemed to have gone.

And we were slowly playing with the minibar like it was a minibar on the Titanic and we were divers from some crazy museum.

And he told me that someone had made a terrible mistake.

Someone had recommended someone with the same name as me to Crawford. Someone at his rugby club.

And they'd made the mistake of giving me the job.

Because they saw my CV first.

But I knew something like this was bound to happen.

He was apologizing, saying it was a monumental cock-up.

And he'd only just found out.

But he eyed me steadily while he told me that if I did anything stupid like trying to sue him, the minute I met his lawyers I'd be dead in the water.

And I hadn't a chance.

I waved my hand limply.

We were both really out of it.

And he kept saying, "Good man. Good man."

And I'd be reimbursed for my inconvenience.

It was just that they'd thought I was somebody else.

He stood at the wall.

And his wife kept ringing the room to see if he was ready to go out for dinner.

And he told me his mother had died a few months ago and she wanted, in her will, for some photo of herself to be sent to some man who used to be their next door neighbor.

He couldn't rest anymore, he said, thinking about it.

"But I suppose," he said, "the past is over, isn't it?"

Later on they were all gone out to dinner and I was on the phone, trying to find out how I could fly back to Dublin.

But I can't remember too much of all this, understandably, because it was all very much like some dream I was having.

There's no way of saying it even without it all seeming very strange to me.

But, like O'Hagan says, the past is over.

Isn't it?

12

JOE

In those days a lot of us could just about boil an egg. Those of us who worked a lot.

There just wasn't the time.

There just wasn't the need.

Breakfast with the kids.

Soup and sandwiches at your lunch.

And off home to your shepherd's pie or your few chops for your tea. Sure you spent half your time trying to get it into the kids, any way you could.

So when they found a cyst on one of Liz's ovaries and the date was set for her to go in and have it done, it was decided that Dermot and Tania would stay with Liz's sister, Aunty Carmel, in Baldoyle.

We drove Liz up to the Bons on a Sunday.

We went into her little room and the kids sat on the bed while she took her few bits out of her overnight bag and got into her nightie.

And pretty soon the sister came in to say the specialist was on his way.

So we all gave Liz a kiss and I drove the kids up to Baldoyle.

Aunty Carmel gave us some mushroom omelets and chips.

And when I left them there, there were no tears or no messing.

This was an adventure for the kids there with their cousins.

Sleeping in their cousins' beds and everything.

And I went home and ran a bath.

I'd barely seen Marion or Tommy Ross since their party.

Which was probably a mistake in itself though.

Because, because I'd gotten a land for myself that night in the kitchen with Marion, and if you don't see the person and see all their little ways that make them normal, you sort of, involuntarily romanticize them, don't you?

It was like the next door neighbors' house was like some kind of bizarre memorial or something.

To what, I don't know.

Some strange dream or the constant possibility that you can
get yourself a bit of a land for yourself, maybe.

And our house felt fierce empty in the morning.

And I phoned Aunty Carmel and spoke to the kids and ate
some bread and butter and tea.

And you know the way sometimes you go to work, but
everything's different and there's a calmness in you that you
didn't think it was possible for you to have?

A strange floaty day.

I suppose because your normal routine is that bit upset.

I left a little early and went up to the Bons where Liz was
fasting.

She was in good form and more looking forward to getting it
over with than afraid.

She was a real Dublin spirit.

And I spoke to the specialist, Mr. Ellis, and we were all very
businesslike all of a sudden, but it was time to go and I
dropped a load of chocolate off up to Aunty Carmel's for
the kids and the cousins.

But they were all out the back playing on a swing
they'd made from one of the trees, and they hardly paid me
any notice so I drove off home.

And there I was, sitting there watching the news and thinking about maybe opening a tin of beans or maybe nipping out for a fish and chip, when perhaps you might say inevitably, the door bell rang, and there was Marion with a plateful of dinner with tinfoil over it.

Which, of course, as a Christian you have to appreciate but because as well this person has reached mythic proportions in your sense of what's right and wrong and what can tip the balance into some kind of unpredictable insanity, you take the plate with slight trepidation, don't you?

But of course she was completely innocent of anything as, technically, we both were.

And she actually stood at the sink and did my breakfast dishes while I ate this food that was very alien to me, and I didn't quite know what it was.

And she was inquiring after Liz and how we were all coping.

And I was trying to work out if she'd done anything to her appearance before dropping in.

Anything to make herself in any way more appealing than she otherwise might've needed to.

And I was sitting there, deciding she hadn't, she was wearing Scholl sandals and a scarf on her head.

And she suddenly stopped and said, "Is that bay rum?" which was something I usually used in my hair in those days.

I said, yes, it was.

And she was slightly miles away, like the smell or me or both
or whatever reminded her of something.

And before she left she said she'd keep an eye on me and if
there was anything I needed done, washing or anything, just
to give her a shout.

And why I felt so bad without having done or said anything
bad, it was awful.

And I was afraid of my life, that I'd be punished somehow
by Liz's operation going awry in some way or that God
was telling me he was taking her away because I was really
supposed to be with somebody else.

But, she was fine and clean as a whistle when I went in to see
her the next evening and Mr. Ellis was confident she'd be
home within the week.

Which I took as a sign that everything was all right and
normal in the world and not to be giving myself heart
attacks over nothing.

But it was a fine, bright April evening and Marion and
Tommy Ross called in to see how Liz was getting on and did
I want my dinner.

They had a little white dog with them on a leash and they
were going for a walk and asked me if I'd like to join them,
but I felt so full of loss looking at Marion pulling at the dog's
leash that I had to say no.

And Tommy told me to call into them for a nightcap later
and I said I would because I needed to get the door shut so
I could lean against the wall.

With like this image of Marion looking down at the little dog and pulling at the leash, her elbow going up, emblazoned into my eyes or something.

And I sat on the stairs and actually watched the house get dark before I got up and went next door.

For a nightcap.

Tommy brought me in and we chatted about various things, like work and politics.

And Marion was upstairs with one of the kids who was getting a bit of a temperature.

But she soon came down and had a Bacardi and Coke with us and I was about to push off, because I felt I needed a few stiffeners at home to sort myself out.

And their little boy came down and he wasn't well and Tommy brought him back up and Marion went to see if she had the number of the doctor.

And for a minute I was alone there in their living room and I was staring at a bookcase and I saw this black-and-white picture of Marion when she was like only a child. But she looked exactly the same.

And she was grinning into the camera with a look halfway between innocence and a dawning mischief that there were things in the world you could get away with.

And I picked it up and I tried to put it in my pocket.

71

And Marion came back in, and basically she caught me.

I pretended I was just wiping it on my jacket, like it was a bit dusty or something.

And I was sort of going, "Is this you? Ha ha ha."

But she had a cold, serious look in her eyes and she just said to me, "Do you want that?"

And I was like, "What? Are you mad? What do you mean? Ha ha ha."

But she was just, "Do you want that?"

And I didn't know what to say.

And she said, "You can have it if you want it."

She said, "You can keep that. If you want it."

And she was so calm about it in a way that I couldn't understand that I nearly did. I nearly took it.

But of course all your dead relatives and teachers from your youth and all the things that are basically yourself are all there, aghast, and I just put it back on the bookcase.

And I went towards the door which meant that I went past her brown shoulder and out into the garden and back into my house where I lay curled up on the sofa, half expecting a soft knocking at the front door or the window which never came.

And I knew that I couldn't take that photograph because I was afraid to. And I was afraid to because I didn't know why I wanted it.

And I felt like that was the truth.

And I barely ever saw or spoke to that woman again.

For better or for worse. Or both, mmm?

Because that's what you do.

13

KEVIN

Predictably by about one o'clock in the morning panes of glass were broken in the living room door.

The guards had already been once to tell us to keep the racket down.

An ambulance had been because some poor eejit had gotten a hiding on his way to the party and he arrived with his nose all over his face.

There was another fight brewing in the front garden between the local hardchaws and a load of crusties who hung out in town.

They were fucking beer cans at each other across the street.

Speedy had fallen asleep in the toilet and the door was locked. Davy finally had to kick it in so the girls could have somewhere to have a slash.

The boys were all just doing it in the garden.

The smell of cider piss out the back was all over the neighborhood. It was like vinegar and the grass was all dead.

There was just a mad atmosphere.

Davy opened up his plastic dustbin full of homebrew.

It was supposed to ferment for two months.

But he'd only started making it on Tuesday and everyone was milling it.

Someone's dad was at the party, standing in the hall, calm as you like, drinking a can of Royal Dutch and talking to this really boring American guy who always seemed to turn up everywhere.

A girl fell down the stairs and people were saying we were going to have to call another ambulance.

And even though me and Clare had locked our bedroom doors there were people in them, and it wasn't worth the hassle trying to get them out.

We were all past caring.

I was standing in the back garden.

Someone had just handed me a goldfish in a little plastic bag full of water.

Unbelievably it was still alive.

No one knew where it came from.

There'd nearly been a mill when one of Clare's old flames had tried to headbutt Declan, her new boyfriend.

But it was over pretty quickly with Clare tearing into your man, screaming insults into his face until he just stood on his own over at the kitchen door, hanging his head in an unbelievable wave of shame.

A little while before I'd seen Trish's curly hair under the oil tank. She was snogging this guy in a big woolly hat. And then she stood up and turned and saw me and I totally believed her as she staggered away saying, "I thought that was you!" Her hands up to her face, starting to laugh.

The chap under the oil tank reached up to her and let out an indistinguishable, "Ughhh . . ." protesting to her. And she just turned and gave him the most almighty kick in the face I've ever seen. He was too drunk to feel it and he was asleep immediately.

It was that type of atmosphere.

Scampi had pulled Davy's amp out into the garden and he was trying to persuade The Bangers to crank up and do a few songs.

And suddenly a football appeared and there was an impromptu game in full swing with no teams and no goal-posts, just loads of random boots and people running around with a mad sense of purpose.

I went over to the side of the house and stood in the passage
to protect the little fish.

I kicked some full cans of Scrumpy in the darkness and
I started to drink them.

Some girl tried to snog me for a minute but I was rapidly
becoming just generally incapable.

And someone ran up to me and said, "Paul McCartney's
actually here!"

And I suddenly felt like there was just nowhere to go.

And the police arrived again and soon it was all over.

Davy was nearly arrested, only Clare intervened on his
behalf saying he was mentally ill.

And I just basically stayed up in the garden all night
wandering around drinking from various cans that were
scattered about.

And when it was bright I went up to my room to have
a sleep but there were people there already.

So I tapped on Clare's door and went in.

She lay on her side, her eyes were open.

Declan was asleep with his arm round her.

I sat down beside the bed with her looking at me.

And I gave her a look that said, "Well, that's that."

And she smiled and she slowly got up to put some clothes on, her brown skin shining in the morning light.

And went downstairs, not saying anything and we went for a walk.

We walked down the Malahide Road, down to Fairview.

Down the Alfie Byrne Road, down past Sheriff Street, down by the Point and across the toll bridge, down to Ringsend.

Down through Sandymount, on out past Booterstown, into Blackrock, down through Monkstown and out into Dun Laoghaire where we walked out onto the harbor wall.

I looked into the bag but the fish had died.

And we walked down the harbor in silence.

Sometimes Clare seemed to take my hand like maybe she wanted to go back.

But I kept going. And she stayed with me.

We'd have to go back soon anyway.

We were running out of land to walk on.

It was just miles and miles of sea.

There was just nowhere left to go anymore.

Except just sort of towards each other for a while.

"What did I say?" My dad said.

"What did I say?"

I was tucking into a bit of Sunday dinner.

"I give it a month! That's what I said. What did I say?"

And to tell you the truth I didn't mind him having his little moment of triumph.

It was a relief, back home, with my mum and dad and my sisters.

My room was just as I'd left it, only tidy, and with clean sheets. And I slept for fifteen hours that night.

And a few nights later Clare called down and we sat in the kitchen drinking cups of tea, listening to the radio.

She was going mad, she said. Back with the folks.

All evening about how it was doing her head in.

But I knew where it was all going.

She was moving out into another house.

With Declan and some of his mates in their band.

And I was sitting there, telling her that this was a great idea.

And there was just something stopping us talking about each other properly. To each other.

Fear? Bewilderment? Disbelief maybe?

That this couldn't be it.

That two people couldn't have found each other this easily.

We didn't trust it I suppose.

So that was that.

And we soldiered on off down our different roads.

A few weeks later my granny died.

My dad's mum.

And I was sitting there at the funeral, watching my grandad holding these rosary beads that had belonged to her, that she'd got from Lourdes.

And I was thinking that maybe there isn't a soul for every person in the world.

Maybe there's just two.

One for people who go with the flow, and one for all the people who fight.

Maybe lots of us just share a soul.

So there's no judgment, because there's no point.

It was just this stupid idea.

But it was in my head like a block or something.

Curly-haired Patricia was there with me at the funeral.

I'd been getting on the bus a lot recently, spending a lot of time down there in Parliament Street.

And later on we were in the pub.

And I was staring down at the tiles on the floor.

Because I knew that she was a fighter, and I had the other soul.

And it was more than just a sneaky suspicion that if she was going to fight for me, that I was going to go with the flow.

14

DERMOT

Understandably, I felt like a man who'd been shot up into the air and all the lads with the nets had fucked off.

And I was coming down to Earth.

Down to Dublin.

Down the back of the plane in economy.

I was like a zombie.

Standing there outside the airport waiting on a taxi.

And when I got one your man is very much on for a big chat.

Where had I been? How was it? What did I do for a living myself?

Holy fuck. I was like one of those figures you see in the religious paintings where God is pointing for them all to go to Hell. And they're all looking up at him, very much feeling the reality of their situation.

I lugged my suitcase into the hall and I could see Mary and Colm out the back garden.

They'd pulled the kitchen table out on the grass so they could have their lunch in the sun.

I took a chair and went out and joined them.

We had ham and boiled eggs and brown bread and tea and a jug of Miwadi orange.

Colm started kicking a ball around but I didn't have the energy.

I just sat there and told Mary the job was gone.

That it was a mistake.

She laughed at me in a way I understood.

That it was inevitable that things like that should happen to me. That I was someone to whom things happened.

Colm came over for a drink of orange and absentmindedly his arm was on the back of my chair and I could hear him slurping his drink and he absentmindedly ran one of his fingers over the stubble on my cheek.

And that he felt entitled to do that held no humiliation for me anymore, I was too tired, and he was gone anyway.

All the little wars you can fight.

All I had to do to level the playing field was put some
chocolate in front of my wife.

And gradually elevate myself in the world.
And Mary just said to me:

"When I met you, do you know why I chose you?
Because I felt sorry for you.
You looked so woebegon that none of the girls would dance
with you.
You looked so scared there with all the other boys.
And remember. I was no mean looker in them days,
Dermot, I had long legs and I had big boobs and a big
blondy dye job in my hair.
And all the boys you were standing there with, they couldn't
believe me walking past them and asking you to dance.
Sure you couldn't believe it yourself!
'What?' You said to me.
You fucking eejit.
What!
I nearly had to drag you to your feet.
You were shaking there on the dance floor.
You were shaking in my arms.
When I planted a kiss on you, you didn't know what to do.
You got the hang of it.
But it took you a minute.
You held onto me like you were afraid you were going to
wake up and I'd be gone.
I'd been with loads of fellas before you.
But they were all obvious for me.
They all had a smart mouth because their mammies had

turned them into mickey dazzlers telling them the sun,
moon and stars shone out of their heads.
But I shut them up.
Because I wasn't a girl who was afraid to put her hand down
a boy's underpants.
I could make a boy do anything I wanted.
But I chose you, Dermot, because you were alone in the
world.
And I knew you probably would be for the rest of your life
and I decided that I was going to be your friend.
And I know you don't think much of me anymore.
And I don't care you take me for granted and I know
I embarrass you because I never lost all this weight after
Colm.
But I chose you Dermot.
I took you because I knew you'd always need someone to
look after you.
And I always will,"
she said.

And it was like I was looking at the three of us there in the
garden from high above.

I could see Colm banging an orange football around down
there against the concrete walls.

And I could see me and Mary sitting there at the table.

Her hand was on the back of my head.

And I was like a hunched figure.

My face falling slowly into her lap.

15

JOE

When you live in close proximity to people in a home like me,
and you're fairly private, you don't let on if you've got news.

Especially if it's of a highly personal nature.

So to look at me walking around with this photo in my
pocket you wouldn't know a thing.

But Sister Pat clocked me a few times, that I was miles away.

And I had to get out of her gaze.

Jackie Fennel thought it was bloody Christmas when
I suggested we go and get a bottle of stout at one o'clock in
the afternoon.

And then Mary Larkin got in on the act.

And of course it was a big event now and everyone was
clucking around that the three of us were turning into
alcoholics.

But what can you do?

So there we were hobbling 'round to Tighe's in the sunshine.

Jackie was the most agile.

He could still do two things at once.

He was counting out his change, not needing to look where he was going.

Mary Larkin was going on about what a beautiful day it was but that didn't stop her ducking into Tighe's where it was all suitably dark and empty, and drinking five bottles of Harp.

She was buckled by half two.

We had the place to ourselves.

Jackie kept fiddling with the telly, looking for the racing, until the barman gave in and let him have the remote control.

And although I was joining in the general conversation, I was secretly in a world of my own.

Thinking about Marion Ross and why she'd had this picture sent to me.

I'd had a look in Jackie's backlog of *Independent*s and I was right.

She'd passed away a few weeks before.

And I was thinking that she was right in a way.

If I wanted a picture of her, why shouldn't I have it?

And if you can be friends, what are you afraid of?

Except of course what had happened was that I'd fallen in love with someone I didn't know and that was all there was about it.

And I never knew her, but when it hits you, it just does.

And maybe if I'd gotten to know her I mightn't even have liked her, but there you are. I know it exists.

But, I made a decision and your life runs its course.

Maybe I could've battled my way around to us ending up together.

But what can I say?

It just wasn't in me.

I'm just not made like that.

And a few bottles of stout and two or three balls of malt later we made our way back around to the home.

Mary Larkin was singing "You Are My Sunshine, My Only Sunshine," but she shut up when Sister Pat hoved into view.

Jackie Fennel was doing a little dance and rubbing his hands together.

"We're home from the fields!" he says to Sister Pat.

And we sat down and had our dinner.

And of course we were the talk of the bloody town.

"Who's birthday was it?" and all this.

Poor Mary had to hit the sack around seven o'clock.

But Jackie was taking them all on.

He was in great form, slagging them all off.

But then, suddenly, he was fading fast.

And Sister Pat put him to bed.

And I sat there on my own in the dining room.

They didn't think anyone was in there so the lights were off.

But Sister Pat came and found me and we went down to her room and had a cup of tea.

And although she was furious I hadn't told her what I'd gotten in the post, the problem was that she liked me too much to give me a hard time.

So we just chatted about this and that and she told me all about where she'd grown up in Roscommon.

And soon enough it was time for bed.

And when I had my pajamas on I went over to the table and took these rosary beads out that used to belong to Liz that she'd gotten in Lourdes.

And I had them sort of wrapped around my fingers.

And naturally I took Marion's photograph out of my jacket and I looked at it for a little while.

This little girl staring up out at me.

A big smile on her.

Very happy.

Someone I didn't know.

And I was slightly too knackered to finish the last couple of pages of this cowboy book I was reading.

So I just lay back with Marion's picture in one hand and Liz's rosary beads in the other.

Thinking about regret and worry.

And when you get to my age, you give up on them because they don't help anything.

And you generally get tired of regret.

And you're usually just whacked out from worrying.

So I brought these two things together on my chest.

The picture and the beads.

On my heart if you like.

And I did what any Christian would do.

I turned out the light and I went to sleep.

CONOR MCPHERSON was born in Dublin in 1971 and attended University College Dublin, where he began to write and direct. He co-founded the Fly by Night Theatre Company, which performed new plays in Dublin's fringe venues.

Published plays include *Rum and Vodka*; *The Good Thief*, which won a Stewart Parker Award; *This Lime Tree Bower*, which won a Thames TV Award, a Guinness/National Theatre Ingenuity Award and the Meyer-Whitworth Award; *St. Nicholas*; *The Weir*, which won the Most Promising Playwright Award from both the *Evening Standard* and the Critics' Circle, and the Laurence Olivier Award for Best Play, ran for eighteen months in the West End of London and played successfully on Broadway; and *Dublin Carol*.

His script for *I Went Down* won Best Screenplay at the San Sebastian Film Festival. *Saltwater*, which he wrote and directed, won numerous European awards, including the CICAE Award for Best Film at the Berlin Film Festival.